MUSICAL
INSTRUMENTS

Drums

Cynthia Amoroso,
Robert B. Noyed,
and John Willis

LET'S READ
AV2
BY WEIGL
ADDED VALUE · AUDIO VISUAL

www.av2books.com

LET'S READ
AV²
BY WEIGL™
ADDED VALUE • AUDIO VISUAL

Go to **www.av2books.com**, and enter this book's unique code.

BOOK CODE

M 8 2 4 5 4 4

AV² by Weigl brings you media enhanced books that support active learning.

E
786.9
AMO

AV² provides enriched content that supplements and complements this book. Weigl's AV² books strive to create inspired learning and engage young minds in a total learning experience.

Your AV² Media Enhanced books come alive with...

 Audio
Listen to sections of the book read aloud.

 Video
Watch informative video clips.

 Embedded Weblinks
Gain additional information for research.

 Try This!
Complete activities and hands-on experiments.

 Key Words
Study vocabulary, and complete a matching word activity.

 Quizzes
Test your knowledge.

 Slide Show
View images and captions, and prepare a presentation.

... and much, much more!

Published by AV² by Weigl
350 5th Avenue, 59th Floor New York, NY 10118
Website: www.av2books.com

Library of Congress Control Number: 2017936393

ISBN 978-1-4896-6004-6 (hardcover)
ISBN 978-1-4896-6005-3 (softcover)
ISBN 978-1-4896-6006-0 (multi-user eBook)

Printed in the United States of America in Brainerd, Minnesota
1 2 3 4 5 6 7 8 9 0 21 20 19 18 17

042017
310117

Project Coordinator: John Willis   Designer: Nick Newton

Weigl acknowledges Getty Images, Alamy, Shutterstock, Dreamstime, and iStock as the primary image suppliers for this title.

MUSICAL INSTRUMENTS

Drums

In this book, you will learn about

drums

what they are

how you play them

and much more!

3

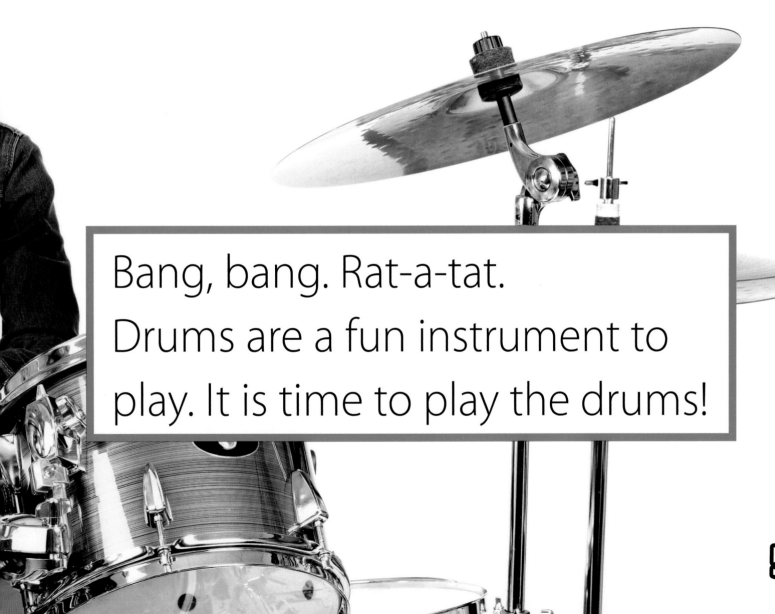

Bang, bang. Rat-a-tat.
Drums are a fun instrument to
play. It is time to play the drums!

Drums can be shaped like many things. A drum can look like a tube or a barrel. A drum can even look like a goblet.

7

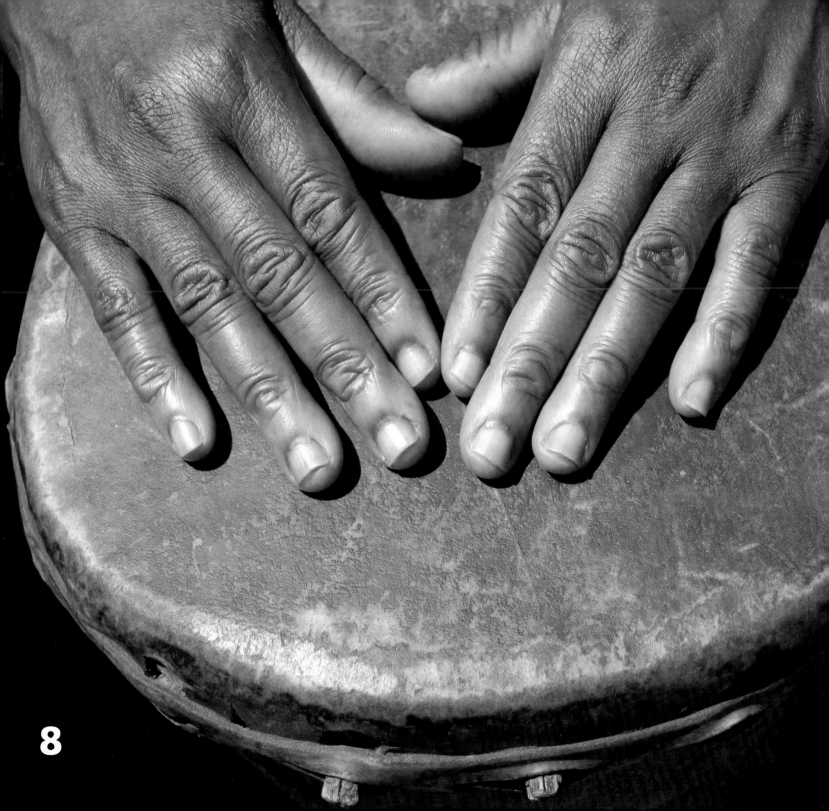

Some drums are big. Some are small. They are made out of many things. Drums can be made out of metal, wood, leather, and plastic.

The first plastic drumheads were invented about 60 years ago.

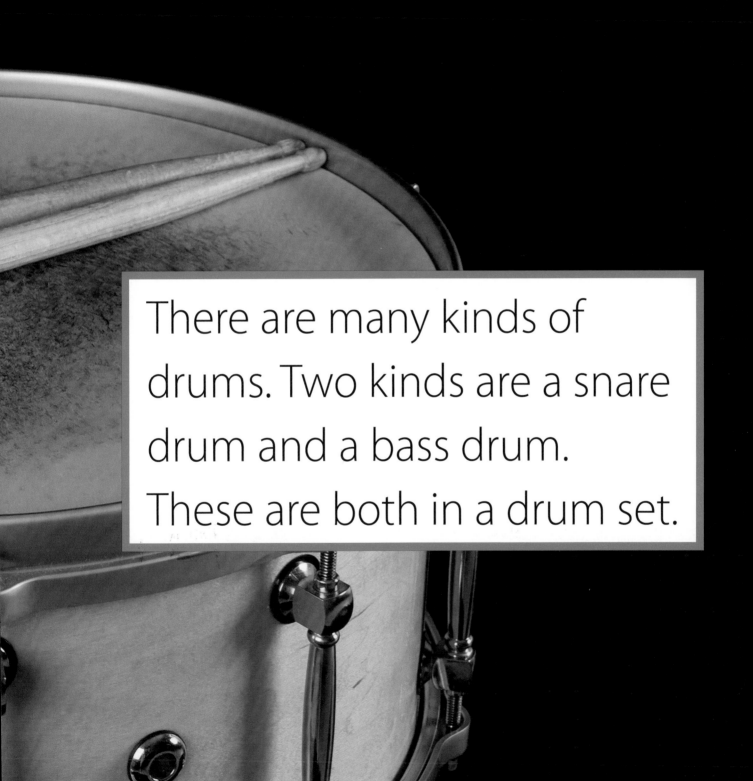

There are many kinds of drums. Two kinds are a snare drum and a bass drum. These are both in a drum set.

Drums have been around for many years. Long ago, people sent messages with drums. Sometimes, armies used drums to help soldiers.

One of the oldest drums ever found was more than 8,000 years old.

13

14

Today, most people use drums to make music. People all over the world play drums. Drum playing is important in many places.

15

People play drums to make a beat. Drumbeats help other instruments play together. Beats can go fast or slow.

Some drums make musical sounds. The sounds can be loud or soft. The notes can be low or high.

You can hit drums with drumsticks or with your hands. Some people use their feet to make sounds, too.

The first drumsticks to use nylon tips were invented in 1958.

See what you have learned about drums.

Which of these pictures does not show a drum?

KEY WORDS

Research has shown that as much as 65 percent of all written material published in English is made up of 300 words. These 300 words cannot be taught using pictures or learned by sounding them out. They must be recognized by sight. This book contains 69 common sight words to help young readers improve their reading fluency and comprehension. This book also teaches young readers several important content words, such as proper nouns. These words are paired with pictures to aid in learning and improve understanding.

Page	Sight Words First Appearance
5	a, are, is, it, play, the, time, to
6	be, can, even, like, look, many, or, things
9	about, and, big, first, made, of, out, small, some, they, were, years
11	both, in, kinds, set, there, these, two
12	around, been, ever, for, found, have, help, long, more, old, one, people, sometimes, than, used, was, with
15	all, important, make, most, over, places, world
16	go, other, together
19	high, sounds
20	feet, their, too, you, your

Page	Content Words First Appearance
5	drums, instrument
6	barrel, goblet, tube
9	drumheads, leather, metal, plastic, wood
11	bass drum, snare drum
12	armies, messages, soldiers
15	music
16	drumbeats, beat
19	notes
20	drumsticks, nylon tips